We Are the Beloved

Other Books by Ken Blanchard

The One Minute Manager (with Spencer Johnson)

Management of Organizational Behavior, 6th ed.
(with Paul Hersey)

The Power of Ethical Management
(with Norman Vincent Peale)

Raving Fans (with Sheldon Bowles)

Organizational Change through Effective Leadership,
2d ed. (with Paul Hersey and
Robert H. Guest)

Putting the One Minute Manager to Work
(with Robert Lorber)

Leadership and the One Minute Manager
(with Drea Zigarmi and Patricia Zigarmi)

*The One Minute Manager Builds High Performance
Teams* (with Don Carew and
Eunice Parisi-Carew)

The One Minute Manager Meets the Monkey
(with William Oncken and Hall Burrows)

The One Minute Manager Gets Fit
(with D. W. Edington and
Marjorie Blanchard)

Playing the Great Game of Golf

We Are the Beloved

the

Beloved

A SPIRITUAL JOURNEY

KEN BLANCHARD

ZondervanPublishingHouse
Grand Rapids, Michigan

A Division of HarperCollins*Publishers*

We Are the Beloved
Copyright © 1994 Ken Blanchard

Requests for information should be addressed to:
Zondervan Publishing House
Grand Rapids, MI 49530

ISBN 0-310-48820-6

Edited by Lyn Cryderman

Cover design by Mark Veldheer

Printed in the United States of America

94 95 96 97 98 99 00 / ❖ DC / 10 9 8 7 6 5 4 3 2 1

This edition is printed on acid-free paper and meets the American
National Standards Institute Z39.48 standard.

This book is dedicated to:
Dorothy Blanchard
Bob Buford
Phil Hodges
Bill Hybels
Norman Vincent Peale

My mom has always been a beautiful spirit and had great faith in the Lord. At ninety-one, she remains an inspiration—a spiritual guide for me and everyone whose life she touches.

When we were working together on *The Power of Ethical Management,* Norman Vincent Peale kept telling me, "Ken, the Lord has always had you on His team; you just haven't suited up yet." Bob, Phil, Bill, and Norman played key roles in my suiting up. I will be talking about them throughout this little book.

This past Christmas Eve, Norman Vincent Peale passed away quietly at ninety-five. He was at home surrounded by love, peace, and tender care. Norman deserved nothing less. His positive thinking ministry made a difference in my life and the lives of generations of people who were profoundly influenced by his sermons, speeches, radio shows, television appearances, and books. While he never got to read this book, Norman's whole life was the life of the beloved.

INTRODUCTION

A number of years ago I started emphasizing the importance of self-esteem in my leadership and management lectures and seminars. I did this because it was becoming clearer to me that managers today, in a world demanding an empowered work force, have to be more like cheerleaders, supporters, and encouragers than the judges, critics, and evaluators they have been in the past. Yet I realized that it is almost impossible for people who don't feel good about themselves to play these new roles. I began to wonder if effective leadership doesn't actually begin on the inside and move out. After all, only people who genuinely like themselves can build up others without feeling it takes something away from themselves.

My sudden concern with self-esteem coincided with a renewed spiritual interest. In confronting my own spirituality, I began to sense that maybe the quickest and most powerful way to significantly enhance one's self-esteem and make ourselves more loving people is a spiritual awakening.

I say "awakening" because I have come to believe that all of us develop amnesia after we are born. We begin to forget from where we came. We start to lose touch with home base. I recently read a beautiful story about a little girl by the name of Sachi. The story is all about this amnesia. Soon after her brother was born, little Sachi began to ask her parents to leave her alone with the new baby. They worried that like most four-year-olds, she might feel jealous and want to hit or shake him, so they said "No." But she showed no signs of jealousy. She treated the baby with kindness, and her pleas to be left alone with him became more urgent. They decided to allow it.

Elated, she went into the baby's room and shut the door, but it opened a crack—enough for her curious parents to peek in and listen. They saw little Sachi walk quietly up to her baby brother, put her face close to his and say quietly, "Baby, tell me what God feels like. I'm starting to forget."

It takes us different lengths of time to get back home—to accept that we come from the best lineage there is and have the unconditional love of the Father—the Master of the House.

This book is not about persuading you to believe in God. I think most people believe in God. Not to believe in a Creator makes as much sense as saying the unabridged dictionary is the result of an explosion in a print shop. My hope is to clear up your amnesia and help you to remember what you once knew in childlike innocence: that there is something or someone out there bigger than you who has a divine purpose for your life. The first step in any spiritual journey is a longing for home; a yearning to reconnect with something bigger than you.

The focus in this book is on "suiting up"—deliberately accepting on faith God's unconditional love for us as manifested in His gift of grace. In sports, you "suit up" when it's time to play. Once you get in uniform, you still might not get sent into the game, but you're ready if the coach needs you. In my travels, I find that most people today are restless and hungry to get "into the game" and experience the deeper meaning of their lives. They just don't know where to start.

Rather than trying to persuade you what to do, I'd simply like to share what I believe is an incredibly good deal. It answers the questions about self-esteem once and for all, for it's the realization that once you receive the Lord's forgiveness through grace, you have all the love you will ever need. No amount of striving for approval or achieving greater and greater things will give you more love and acceptance than you already have.

That's why I titled this book *We Are the Beloved*—because you already are loved, with no strings attached.

Even if you decide that you cannot yet accept God's love, you are still loved by Him. You just miss out on having the most important teammate you could ever have.

This deal is also incredibly good because it satisfies our longing for meaning and purpose. It lends to everyday life a quality that I think most of us are desperate for today—the sense that we're on our own hero's journey, that spiritually speaking, life can be viewed as a magic carpet ride.

This little book was originally written as a Christmas 1994 gift for the most important people in my life—my family and friends. It is through their urging that I agreed to share the story of my spiritual journey more widely. I share it not because I think it is so extraordinary. In fact, I'm still en route, with much yet to learn. Sometimes we teach what we most need to learn. I needed to write this book as much for me as for you.

I feel like the rabbi who went to live in a corrupt city. Every day he ran through the streets of the city and shouted over and over, "Repent! Turn from your sins. Repent! Turn from your sins." Days led into weeks and weeks led into months and months led into years. Every day the rabbi could be heard shouting his plea. Finally one day a friend asked the rabbi, "No one listens to you;

everyone is laughing at you; why do you continue to do this?"

The rabbi was quick to reply: "When I first came here I dreamt of a city turned toward God. I envisioned the city changing. That has not happened, so today I run through the streets shouting my plea to keep the city from changing me."

This book is a meditation about God's unconditional love. I hope it helps you to think seriously about accepting this love, together with all the self-esteem, power, and freedom which it brings. But if that does not happen, all is not lost.

I still need the message myself.

—KEN BLANCHARD
FALL 1994

We Are the Beloved

My Journey

The grace of our Lord
was poured out on me abundantly,
along with the faith and love
that are in Christ Jesus.

<small>1 Timothy 1:14</small>

grew up in New Rochelle, New York. Bob Hartley was the pastor of the First Presbyterian Church my parents attended, and his ministry had such a big impact on them that when I was born they gave me the middle name Hartley. I never got to know Bob Hartley; he died of a heart attack when I was five. But in later years I learned that my coauthor and friend, Norman Vincent Peale, had been a classmate of Reverend Hartley at divinity school.

Over the years my mom has repeatedly told me a story about Bob Hartley that will give you a sense of the kind of person he was. As background, my father attended the Naval Academy at Annapolis, Maryland. When he graduated in 1924 he found that in a world that believed it had just fought the "war to end all wars," there was little need for naval officers. So, after a senior cruise, he entered Harvard Business School, where he majored in finance and ended up working in New York City. In the early 1940s, he was being groomed for a vice-presidency with National City Bank when one day he came home and said to my mom, "Well, honey, I quit today."

"You did what?" my mother replied.

"I quit," Dad said. "I told you when we got married that if the country ever got in trouble, I felt I owed it something. Hitler is already a threat to world peace, and it's only a matter of time until Japan gets into the fray, so I re-enlisted."

This was quite a shock for my mom. Just when Dad was starting to make some good money, he'd opted for a lieutenant's salary in the Navy. But Mom went along with it.

In spite of my father's zest for action, his first assignment was the Brooklyn Navy Yard. Pearl Harbor came along, and still no change. When it looked like he'd be stuck in dry dock for the duration of the war, he called one of his former classmates who was head of the Naval Bureau of Personnel in Washington, D.C., and asked him what he had for an old-timer with no experience. A week later his friend called him back. "Ted, all I have for a guy with your background is a suicide group going into the Marshall Islands."

My dad jumped at it—without telling my mom, of course. They gave him command of twelve LCIs (landing craft infantry). With only small guns to protect themselves, Dad's units were responsible for protecting the marines and frogmen heading into the island beaches that were held down by the Japanese. My dad's friend had been right in calling this a suicide mission; it was one of the most vulnerable positions in the campaign. His ships were so close to the beaches that seventy percent of Dad's men were killed or wounded. Dad's picture was in *Time* magazine one week; it showed him conducting funeral services for some of his men who were hit by explosives that fell short after they were launched from our big ships.

As my dad's ships headed into Saipan for what was expected to be the biggest battle in the Pacific, he wrote to Mom's oldest brother Fred: "Chances of me making it out of this campaign are very slim. I know if anything happens you'll watch over Dorothy and the kids." To my mother he wrote a second letter, telling her: "Everything is fine here on maneuvers. The only trouble we're encountering is the heat."

Through some strange accident of fate, Dad got the two letters mixed up. My uncle got Mom's "maneuvers" letter, and she got the one about the low probability of survival. Devastated, she ran to the phone and called Reverend Hartley. In ten minutes he was at our front door with a big smile on his face.

"What a blessing!" he exclaimed.

Mom thought the reverend had lost his mind. "What do you mean 'what a blessing'?"

"It's God's sign that Ted's going to be okay," he said. "The letters getting mixed up means that we've been getting too complacent and not praying enough."

When I told that story to Norman Vincent Peale, he said, "Now that's good preaching!" Whether it was good preaching or just praying enough, it worked because my dad came home safe and sound.

Soon after the war, Bob Hartley died. We continued to go to the First Presbyterian Church until I was in junior high. Then we moved to the First Methodist Church where a classmate's father, Harrison Davis, was the minister. Not only was he a good preacher, he was a wonderful guy as well.

Throughout high school, I was a regular churchgoer, active in Youth Fellowship. Then I went off to college at Cornell. Under the university's hands-off policy with regard to student religious observances, I started to drift away. With studies and an increasingly busy campus life, I never really found a church to attend in Ithaca.

The summer after I graduated I started to date Margie McKee. We both were working in the Ithaca area. Margie had gone out with a number of my good friends, and they all said she was "the greatest." In fact, I called her for a date as a favor to one of my friends who was concerned she might be lonely.

Margie was a speech therapy major and was working at a special camp for handicapped kids. When I arrived to pick her up, I said, "Tell me what you do out here." She spoke with such love and compassion about her work with those kids that I fell in love with her during the seven-mile ride into town. By the end of the evening I was already worrying about how to tell my friend the "bad news." Margie and I were married a year later, after her graduation from Cornell. My friend named his first child Ken, so he ended up all right too.

The first year we were married we lived in Hamilton, New York, while I finished my master's degree and Margie worked as a speech therapist for the Madison County schools. When we returned to Cornell the next year for my doctorate and Margie's master's degree, we met a fabulous young minister from the First Presbyterian Church in Ithaca by the name of Paul Clark. He got us gung ho for church again, and we even volunteered to run the junior high school program.

In 1966 we headed out to Ohio University in Athens for my first job as administrative assistant to the dean of the College of Business Administration. Our son, Scott, was just a baby, and Margie was pregnant with Debbie. In Athens we met a wonderful minister at the Methodist church in town and began to be active in that church.

This was the late sixties, a time of much student unrest. The Kent State incident occurred right down the road. We had our own little incident of disillusionment that fit right in with the times. Our minister friend sympathized with students; he was right up front at all the protests and marches. That didn't go over well with his conservative southeastern Ohio congregation. They fired him in what seemed to us a most un-Christian manner.

Anger and disillusionment came crashing in on us. We thought, "If that's what church is all about, forget it." We dropped out. Like so many people, we went to church only at Christmas and Easter—for fifteen years.

Unfortunately, since these were the key growing-up years for Scott and Debbie, faith was not a big part of our family's life in Ohio. Nor did things change in that department when we moved to Amherst, Massachusetts, in 1970, where I taught at the University of Massachusetts and Margie worked on her doctorate in communication studies. After several years there, we went to San Diego for a one-year sabbatical. Living in California for a few months where sunshine is cheap, we realized that summer in Massachusetts was two weeks of bad skating. We decided to stay on the west coast and start our own company. In 1979, Blanchard Training and Development, Inc. (BTD), was launched.

Then *The One Minute Manager* happened. Spencer Johnson, my coauthor, and I met at a cocktail party in November 1980. Margie met him first and led him over to me.

Spencer was working on a One Minute Parenting book with a psychiatrist. When he explained his approach to parenting, I told him I had been teaching those kinds of things to managers for years.

So I invited him to a seminar I was giving the following Monday at the Ranch Bernardo Inn in San Diego. He came and sat in the back of the room and laughed throughout the day. At the end of the seminar he ran up to me and said, "Forget parenting! Let's go for managers." That was the birth of *The One Minute Manager*.

We had a first draft ready for people to read in a Winnebago on the way to the Rose Bowl on December 31. We self-published *The One Minute Manager* by May 1981 and introduced it at the National Restaurant Association Convention in Chicago later that month. Dick Gaven, a friend and fraternity brother of mine, was the Director of Education for the association and got us on the program. Within twenty minutes after the session we had sold almost a thousand copies of the book in the back of the room. During the next year, with almost no publicity, we sold 20,000 copies, mainly to our Blanchard Training and Development customers.

When Spencer and our literary agent, Margaret McBride, went to New York for meetings in January 1982, they found that many publishers were interested in the book. Two weeks after its publication by William Morrow in September, it was on the *New York Times* best-seller list, where it stayed for the next three years.

Several months after the book was out I got a call from Phil Hodges, a longtime friend from Cornell, wanting to know if we could get together for a walk on the beach. Phil was a top labor-relations officer for Xerox, working in the Los Angeles area. When we took our walk, Phil asked, "Ken, why do you think *The One Minute Manager* is such a runaway best-seller? Is it that you're a better writer than anyone else or that you're smarter than most people?"

I said, "No, Hodge, I don't think that at all. I've thought a lot about it. I think the Lord wanted the book written, and He just used Spencer and me as His channels. When I go back and read the book, I can't even remember writing certain parts of it. The book seemed to write itself."

Phil grinned. "I hoped you would have that kind of attitude."

That meeting with Phil Hodges marked the renewal of my spiritual journey that had begun when I was a little guy being taken to church by my parents. Afterward, Phil kept calling me, sending me things to read, pushing me to think about my relationship with Christ.

In 1985 my journey got a boost when Margie and I met Bob and Linda Buford. Bob was a member of the Young Presidents Organization (YPO). To become a member of YPO you have to become president of your organization before you are forty years old and have a minimum of $5 million in sales or budget and at least fifty people working for you. I'd met Bob casually before at some YPO events where Margie and I had been asked to speak, so I knew of his commitment to a personal ministry to help the ministers of large churches and be a special coach for many business leaders.

On the way to a YPO conference in Mexico City we saw the Bufords between flights in the Admirals Club at the Dallas–Fort Worth Airport. When we got on the plane, I discovered that Bob's seat was across the aisle from mine. Earlier in the day I had found tucked away among the bills in my wallet a little booklet about the spiritual laws of Christianity that Phil Hodges had given to me. His daughter LeeAnne had gotten it at

Sunday school. I don't recall putting it in my wallet, but there it was! Now that Bob Buford was sitting next to me, finding that booklet took on new meaning.

I said, "Bob this booklet is in my wallet for some reason. Maybe it means we should talk about Christianity. I have a few questions I'd like to ask you."

"I'll do my best, Ken," said Bob. "But remember. I'm only a layman."

So there in the sky we started going over the booklet together. The first spiritual law stated: God loves you and offers a wonderful plan for your life.

I could buy that one all right, but the second law was where my questions started. It contended that we are all sinners. That had always bothered me. From my standpoint, the concept of original sin was too negative. I'd always thought that people should be considered to have "original potentiality." That is, as human beings we have the potential to be either good or bad.

When I asked Bob about original sin he said, "Let me ask you a question, Ken. Do you think you're as good as God?"

"Of course not," I answered. "The concept of God has to do with perfection."

"Okay. On a scale of 1 to 100, let's give God 100. We'll give Mother Teresa 90, and an ax murderer 5.

Ken, you're a decent sort and are trying to help others. I'll give you 75. Now the special thing about Christianity is that God sent Jesus to make up the difference between you and 100."

That appealed to me. I'd never heard Christianity explained that way.

"Now a lot of people don't like the fact that the ax murderer gets the same shot at the ball as Mother Teresa," continued Bob, "but that's what grace is all about. It's not about deeds. If you accept Jesus as your Savior, no matter what your past has been, He rids you of your sins and brings you closer to 100."

For the rest of the flight I peppered Bob with questions. As we deplaned in Mexico City, Bob said, "I've got a friend I want you to meet who can answer your questions much better than I can. His name is Bill Hybels, and he's minister of one of the fastest-growing churches in the country, the Willow Creek Community Church outside of Chicago. And another thing—he's speaking at this conference. If it's okay, I'm going to see to it that you guys have lunch together."

Bill Hybels and I did have lunch, and he later described our conversation in his inspirational book *Seven Wonders of the Spiritual World*. I led off with the same question I'd asked Bob Buford: "Why original sin? It's too negative."

Bill said, "Ken, let me explain the difference between Christianity and religion. The main difference is in how they're spelled. Religion is spelled 'do.' That means there are all kinds of things you must do to receive the Lord's grace. Religion stresses what you need to do to deserve God's favor. What new leaf can you turn over? What new commitment can you make to get yourself right with God? The problem with religion and the 'do' philosophy is that most people quit because they never know when enough is enough. Suppose you do 2,500 good things in your life, and then you get to judgment day and the Lord says, 'That's not bad but you needed to do 3,000.'"

Bill went on to say, "Christianity is spelled 'done.' The Lord sent Jesus to earth to take care of it. You can't perform well enough or do enough good things to get into heaven. The only entry is by admitting you are a sinner [that is, falling short of a 100 in Bob Buford's terms] and accepting Jesus as your Savior. He is the only one who can cleanse your past. You *cannot* do it yourself."

Bill talked about a personal relationship with Christ, something I had not experienced even in the days when I was active in church. "Not only can He save you, but He can become your guide and your friend. He can energize your life and transform it."

The simplicity of Bill's explanation hit me. I had attended church for years, but I had never heard the message of grace with such clarity and power. All my misgivings about original sin were stripped away. I wasn't a bad person; I just fell short of God's perfection and only by accepting Jesus as my Savior could I be given grace. Then I could reach 100 and be right with the Lord through God's forgiveness of my imperfections.

When I asked Bill how I could accept grace, he said, "It's easy for a One Minute Manager. All you have to do is bow your head and say, 'Lord, I can't save myself. I am a sinner. I accept Jesus Christ as my Savior and bridge between me and You. From this day forward I turn my life over to Him.'"

While I was excited and could feel the adrenaline pumping, I was reluctant to jump in with both feet. And Bill could sense it. I told him I was worried about a commitment to Christ because I was afraid I wouldn't be able to follow through. "I'll fail."

Bill took out a pen and wrote the words "commit" and "follow through" on a paper napkin. Then he said, "Please don't ever use those two words. Becoming a Christian is not committing and following through. God *knows* you can't keep your commitment. God *knows* you can't follow through. Christianity is a matter of two different words: *receive* and *trust*. Romans 6:23

says, 'For the wages of sin is death, but the free gift of God is eternal life in Jesus Christ our Lord.'"

"What is a gift?" Bill asked.

I said, "Something you receive."

"That's right," said Bill. "Salvation, regeneration, newness of life, and forgiveness of sin are things that can only be received. And once you receive grace, once you receive forgiveness, you've got them. Your next step is to trust God and say, 'I don't know what all this means, and I don't know where I am going, but I am going to trust You each step of the way and see what happens.'"

My lunch with Bill really made me think about Christianity. But I still wasn't ready to "suit up" yet, to use Norman Vincent Peale's term. I just wasn't ready to let go of my life and hand it over to God.

After our lunch together, whenever I saw Bill at the conference he would smile and say, "Receive and trust."

It's hard for human beings to let go completely. We think we can figure everything out for ourselves. I kept on thinking about what Bob and Bill had said, but it wasn't until a year later that I acknowledged I was seriously ready to "suit up."

Meanwhile, Margie and I turned over the presidency of Blanchard Training and Development to an individual who had more business experience than we did and who felt he could move our company forward. As it turned out, we didn't always agree on some basic things. No matter how much we tried to see things as he did, it just didn't help. He had a high need to control and a win-lose attitude toward most things. His approach might have been appropriate in a different organization, but at BTD it was a disaster.

Margie and I tried everything to resolve this conflict, but no matter what we tried, it just didn't help. It became clear that things were just not working out. What was worse, I felt powerless to do anything about it.

One evening, Margie and I decided to meet at a local restaurant for dinner and talk about our options.

Earlier that day, I recalled a conversation I'd had with Bill Hybels. We'd once talked about my work as a consultant, helping executives solve sticky problems that came up in their organizations. Bill had said, "Ken, I can't understand why you won't receive the gift of God's grace, because if you do, you get three top consultants working with you—the Father, who heads it all up, the Son, who lived the examples, and the Holy Spirit, who is your day-to-day operating manager. When you pray to the Father and accept the Son as your Savior, the Holy Spirit jumps in and offers sure guidance whenever you're stuck. Three consultants in one. That's not a bad deal, Blanchard."

As my dinner meeting with Margie approached, I thought, *Man, why am I trying to solve this all by myself?* Suddenly, I knew what I was going to do. A wave of tremendous relief flowed through me. I bowed my head and said, "Lord, I can't save myself here. I can't solve problems like this without Your help. I admit I need You and recognize my vulnerability. I accept Jesus as my Savior and the bridge between You and me." The moment I said these words, a great peace came over me.

That feeling was still with me when I walked into the restaurant to meet Margie. She took one look at me and said, "What happened to you? You look so relaxed and calm." Then I told her what I had done, and how I was going to trust God to give me the wisdom and strength to deal with the problem presented by our president. Later, I phoned Bill Hybels and left a message on his answering machine that I had received Christ and was ready to trust my life to Him.

I would like to report that God solved this business problem with some miraculous stroke of His hand, but it didn't happen that way, and I've learned that it seldom does. Yet I believe His hand was on me when a few days later I attended a meeting of the American Society for Training and Development, at which a friend and colleague, Tom Crum, was speaking. Tom is the author of *The Magic of Conflict* and an expert in aikido, an oriental form of self-defense that stresses using the energy of your opponent to defeat that person. Through Tom's dynamic demonstrations and his way of involving all participants in practice, he showed us how to neutralize an attack by responding in ways other than resisting it.

"If someone goes to punch you," Tom said, "don't try to block the punch. When you do that, you are using resistance—your own power and strength against the attacker's. That sets up a win-lose confrontation." Tom showed how to step aside with an accepting and pivoting movement, using the attacker's energy to throw that person or apply a neutralizing technique. The key for all this, as Tom teaches it, is to learn how to be centered, with both mind and body relaxed and alert. Tom told us, "Never get in front of a fast-moving train. When someone comes at you in anger, step back and try to figure out where the energy is coming from."

After lunch that day, I again met with our president. Fully suited up, I now had the courage to face the issue. I told him I wanted to share some concerns of mine about some incidents that had occurred recently. As I started to talk about these incidents, he suddenly exploded. He screamed, "I've had enough of this. You

31

always believe everybody else. I'm not going to take it anymore. I quit!"

That tremendous calm came over me again, even though our president continued to rant and rave. Finally I said to him, "Well, if that's your decision, then good-bye." I calmly walked out of his office. I never got in front of his fast-moving train. When I suited up, I put on God's armor. I then had the strength to stand aside instead of get in the way. I could admit I had made a mistake in hiring this man. I could be at peace even if letting him go risked having people say the One Minute Manager had fallen on his face.

Our former president had some second thoughts the next day and tried to patch things up, but I stood firm. It was clear he just needed to move on.

Again, it would be tempting to say that God solved this personnel problem, that He rewarded me for accepting Him by setting up the meeting with our president and leading the guy to say, "I quit." But I have come to realize that God doesn't work that way. He is not Santa Claus, inviting us to give Him a wish list so He can hand us everything we want. Instead, He promises us something better when we turn our lives over to Him: that He will be with us always, in the good times and the bad.

At Gethsemane, Christ prayed to His Father that He wouldn't have to go through with the agony of the crucifixion, but that prayer was not granted. If God chose not to save His Son, then why should I expect that He would take on the assignment of solving BTD's personnel problem just because Ken Blanchard turned the problem over to Him?

I believe that instead of solving my personnel problems, God opened my eyes when I surrendered to Him. The reward for suiting up was that I discovered I was not alone—that the new suit I was wearing was a suit of armor. After suiting up, I was able to confront the president calmly and reasonably—something I had not been able to do before because I did not think I was up to it. During the meeting, I stood my ground, where before, I might have given in to his demands because I wanted to be loved, to be the good guy. Now I knew I was already loved and no amount of pleasing others would add to that love. The backbone of God's love was the spine that stood the test when the president returned to ask for his job back.

The real story—the true reward for suiting up—is that I was able to take responsibility for cleaning up my own mess, but I didn't have to go into the battle on my own. Maybe the following imaginary conversation with God will show you what I mean. Sheldon Bowles, my good friend and coauthor of *Raving Fans*, helped me understand this by turning my experience with the president into an imagined conversation with God.

"God, I've got this problem, see . . . and I need to be sure I'm doing the right thing."

"Okay, Ken, I'm with you. It will feel right. You'll know it's the right way."

"Thanks, God. That's a big help. But . . . well, it's tough. I mean to confront that guy and everything. Lend me Your strength."

"No problem, Ken. I'm with you. No matter what happens, remember you're on My team . . . and that means I'm on your team."

"That's great, God. But the guy says he's going to quit. I know that feels right. I trust You that it's right. But wow! This guy's anger has really escalated. I'm way out of my comfort zone here. Give me some strength and peace to make the move."

"Still with you, Ken. Confirm he's going. It's your move. Grab the moment. I'll back you all the way no matter what happens."

"I did it, God. He's gone. But now he wants to come back! That's tough. I trusted You that it was the right thing to do, but at the same time, not to give him a second chance . . . I haven't been perfect either, You know. I'm tempted to let him come back. Give me the courage of my convictions. Give me the strength for this one."

"I'm with you, Ken. I know it hurts. But I'm here all the way. You can do it."

"Thanks, God. You did it. He's gone. Thanks for taking care of him. Thanks for doing it."

"No, Ken. You did it. I was just there to backstop you. To carry you if you fell. I was there to love you even if you failed. Even if you would have made more of a mess, Ken, I would still love you. The fact that you handled this problem right does not make Me love you more. You have all of My love already, Ken. All of it."

Or here's another possible scenario:

"God, I trusted my feelings and let him go, but then I learned that he wasn't doing such a bad job after all. The people I trusted had not been telling the truth about him. I've wronged a good man, God. Sorry, God. Sorry I screwed up."

"I'm sorry too, Ken. Learn from it. I can't say I'm pleased that you weren't more careful. But always remember I love you. Even when you're wrong, Blanchard, I love you."

"Glad to hear that, God. I need to know that because now I've got to go and make amends with the man I drove away. I don't know how I'll face him. Give me the strength, Lord. Stand by me."

"I'm here, Ken. You can do it. You won't be alone. I'm coming too. Let's go."

"One last question, God. You said if it felt right to do it. That I'd know. Well, it felt right and I did it and I was wrong. What happened, God? Why did You let me down?"

"It's called free will, Ken. I don't get directly involved. If I did, what would be the point of your being alive? Yes, I said to trust your feelings about the decision, but sometimes you aren't honest with yourself. Your ego gets in the way. Or you act too fast without thinking. Sometimes you take the easy way out. Remember, though, right or wrong, I love you. If you were perfect, you'd have My job. You can't always be right, but you can care and learn. Now let's go see that president, Ken. You've got a mighty big One Minute Apology ahead of you and it will be tough. But I know you can do it. I'm going to be with you. I always am."

"Thanks, God. Without You in my corner life would be hell."

"Exactly, Ken. That's it exactly."

STAYING ON COURSE

*Blessed is the man
who perseveres under trial,
because when he has stood the test,
he will receive the crown of life
that God has promised
to those who love him.*

JAMES 1:12

hat's the story of my journey; how I came to accept grace. I am still learning what it all means, but it is the best deal around.

Phil Hodges told me one time that to appreciate Christianity and the gift God has given us, you have to recognize the difference between justice, mercy, and grace. With *justice*, if you commit a crime you get the penalty you deserve. With *mercy*, if you commit a crime you are given less punishment than you deserve. With *grace*, someone else has already taken the sentence— taken the punishment you deserve. The Lord loves us so much that He sacrificed His only son, Jesus Christ, to wipe our slate clean and give us the gift of salvation.

While lowering my head and acknowledging that the gift of grace and salvation took only a minute, that was just the beginning. The real question was whether I would continue to believe God's unconditional love. Would I continue to trust my life to Him and see what happens? Would I continue to trust Him to give me the wisdom and strength, or would I go back to fear and not wanting to risk? Would I go back to living life with myself as the center when the newness of my faith wore off? Would I forget about my relationship with the Father and resume thinking I can figure everything out myself?

At the end of my seminars people often come up to me and say, "Ken, I'm committed to being a One Minute Manager. I'm committed to being the kind of manager you described today."

My response is quick: "I'm not concerned about your commitment. But I *am* concerned about your commitment to your commitment." People say diets don't work. Diets work fine. People don't! They keep on breaking their commitment to their commitment.

All of these questions I was having about my newly received faith reflected a lack of confidence in my commitment to my commitment. But as Bill Hybels reminded me, "God already knows we can't keep our commitments, yet He still loves us."

That's so hard for us to understand because as human beings we have difficulty giving up control and believing that *it is already done*. We're led astray by voices in our heads that try to convince us there are still things we must do to deserve the Lord's grace. Boy, would I like a chance to replay some of the things I've done in the last few years! Times when I forgot where home was and let those earthly voices win out.

Jesus Himself faced those same temptations. The inspirational writer Henri Nouwen relates in a humorous and powerful way how Jesus responded to the temptations of the Evil One who said, "Prove that you are beloved. Do something! Change these stones into bread. Be sure that you are famous. Jump from the temple and you will be on TV and grab some power so you will have real influence. Don't you want some influence? Is not that what you came for?" Jesus said, "No! I don't have to prove anything. *I am already the beloved.*"

Why is it that so often we get distracted and off course? Is it because we don't believe that we are the beloved and that the same voice that was talking to Jesus is also talking to us? What's keeping me and others who have already acknowledged grace from trusting God totally and bringing Him into our daily concerns and decisions? Why is it that so many Christians get sidetracked on political or cultural issues to the point that they no longer reflect the love of God? I think it's because we want to feel valuable, worthy, important. The irony is that we are valued and loved by God without doing anything to merit it. All we need to do is open our hearts and minds to the love that awaits us all.

Norman Vincent Peale once told me, "If I were the Lord I would be laughing because I gave people everything they need to make their lives work and then added one little twist at the end: free will. With free will the Lord gave people the capacity to make their lives miserable."

H.E.L.P. for the journey

Given the fact that I am not a robot and have the freedom to choose which direction I turn, how do I keep myself on course? How do I get back on course if I stray?

I have learned to seek H.E.L.P., an acronym that stands for Humility, Excellence, Listening, and Praising. I have found it a useful framework for helping me to remember to trust the Lord and His unconditional love for me. I have found that I stay on course much better when I am:

- Grounded in *humility*
- Focused on my own sense of personal *excellence*—a balance between achieving and connecting
- Quiet and *listening* to the voice that assures me, "You are the beloved"
- Accenting the positive and *praising* God for my progress

Let me share this H.E.L.P. formula with you in more detail:

Humility

"People with humility don't think less of themselves, they just think of themselves less." In that quote from our book *The Power of Ethical Management*, Norman Vincent Peale and I were suggesting that it's healthy to feel good about yourself—but don't get carried away. The problem is with the ego.

Someone once told me that *ego* stands for "edging God out." When we start to get a distorted image of our own importance and see ourselves as the center of the universe, we lose touch with who we really are as children of God. Our thinking blurs, and we lose the sense of our connection with home base, others, and our true selves. Like the little girl trying to talk with her baby brother, we forget what God is like.

There are two types of ego-centeredness: *self-doubt* and *false pride*. Both are enemies of humility. People with self-doubt are consumed with their shortcomings and tend to be hard on themselves. People with false pride think they don't need grace, and are out of touch with their own vulnerability to sinfulness. Both have a hard time believing they are loved.

I have to confess that self-doubt is an area that can easily shove me off course. As a people person, I don't want anyone to disapprove of me. When I read the evaluation comments from my seminar participants or from the readers of my books, even though the overwhelming majority are positive, I tend to focus on the negative ones. It's difficult for me to accept praise. After a successful seminar or speech, I will catch myself saying things like, "It was no big deal." Those words may sound appropriately humble, but with me they come from self-doubt. I may have worked five hours to speak twenty minutes, but I still discount positive feedback. Also, in our company I have had trouble making personnel decisions (as you learned earlier) because I'm uncomfortable when people get upset with me.

It's difficult for people with self-doubt to acknowledge grace. They think they don't deserve it. They fail to realize that God did not make junk. To keep self-doubt from convincing you that you have to achieve God's love, remember that you were made by some pretty good hands. *You are the beloved.*

People with false pride have trouble believing in God, much less accepting Jesus as their Savior. They are unwilling to see their own errors or any difficulties in themselves. The story of Adam and Eve is the story of false pride. The serpent didn't offer them an apple because he thought they wanted some fruit. He played

on their egos, telling Eve, "Your eyes will be opened and

you will be like God" if they would just taste the forbidden fruit.

When our false pride gets in the way, we think we are like God. We lose touch with the fact that we all fall short of 100. We think we deserve *all* the credit, that we're the source of *all* good ideas, that our work is the *most important*, that we don't need the help of others.

It's easy to understand that self-doubt comes from lack of self-esteem, because people afflicted with it on a daily basis act as if they are worth less than others. It is less obvious with people with false pride because they behave as if they are worth more than others. People with false pride who act as if they are the only ones who count are really trying to make up for their own lack of self-esteem. They overcompensate for their "not okay" feelings by trying to control everything and everybody around them. In the process, they make themselves unlovable to those around them.

The last several years I've found myself entangled in some very unpleasant legal hassles with former partners. None of the disputes should have gotten to the point where legal involvement was needed. But I was convinced I was right and they felt they were right. In the process of trying to be right, we all forgot that *we are the beloved*. As a result, in many ways we all lost. Pride clouds our vision. We don't see things clearly, and we have a particularly hard time seeing the other person's point of view. When we suit up and trust God, His love helps heal the blind spots.

So why did these legal hassles come along, even though I had put my trust in God? Shouldn't Christians have easier lives? That's old naive thinking that falsely tells us that if we love God, then everything will go right for us. When we think this way, we get angry when trouble comes our way, and we are tempted to go back to doing things on our own. After all, God let us down.

I have come to learn, however, that when bad things happen, that is the time to learn and grow. In my case, the financial and emotional drain of the legal hassles had a purpose. The Bible says that all quarrels are the result of pride. The Lord needed to knock me over the head so that I could relearn (hopefully for good) that being right is the most useless of human endeavors. The worst thing about having to be right is that you have to find someone to be wrong. That's completely counter to the good news of Christianity and its focus on love. Henri Nouwen again gives us guidance:

> And in the spirit of God the fact that you are chosen and blessed and beloved does not mean that others are less so. In fact, the opposite is happen-

ing when you discover your belovedness. You have an inner eye that allows you to see the belovedness of other people and call that forth. That's the incredible mystery of God's love. The more you know how deeply you are loved, the more you'll see how deeply your sisters and brothers in the human family are loved.

In Gordon MacDonald's book *Ordering Your Private World*, he makes an important distinction between *driven* and *called* people. People who are driven think they own everything—their job, their possessions, their spouses, their kids, and their ideas. As a result, they spend all their time trying to protect what they own. Driven people are constantly calling in the lawyers to set matters right.

On the other hand, people who are called think everything is on loan from God. Since they don't own anything, they figure their role in life is to shepherd everybody and everything that comes their way. In relationships, it means helping to bring the best out in others. Being helpful is more important than being right. Instead of calling in the lawyers, called people are constantly looking to God to set things right.

It's interesting for me to see how self-doubt and false pride play out in managers. When they are addicted to either ego infliction, it erodes their effectiveness.

Managers dominated with self-doubt are often called "do-nothing bosses." They are described as "never around, always avoiding conflict, and not very helpful." They often leave people alone even when they are insecure and don't know what they are doing. They don't seem to believe in themselves or trust in their own judgment. They value others' thoughts more than their own—especially the thoughts of those they report to. As a result, they rarely speak out and support their own people. Under pressure they seem to defer to whomever has the most power.

At the other end of the spectrum are the "controllers." These are managers dominated by false pride. Even when they don't know what they are doing, they have a high need for power and control. Even when it's clear to everyone that they are wrong, they keep on insisting they are right. These folks aren't much for supporting their people either. If everyone is upbeat and confident, the controller throws out the wet blanket. They support their bosses over their people because they want to climb the hierarchy and be part of the boss's crowd.

If any of this sounds a bit too close for comfort, don't be alarmed. Most of us have traces of both self-doubt and false pride, because the issue is really ego. We are stuck, all alone, focusing only on ourselves. The good news of the gospel is that results or approval from others is no longer important. "Done" means just that. Jesus took care of it. If we can accept God's unconditional love, we set the stage for receiving His grace. And when you receive it, your slate is wiped clean.

When you realize that God is in your corner you also know you have all the support, love, and backing you'll ever need. It's a humbling experience. Norman Vincent Peale once told me that bowing your head and admitting you can't save yourself is the toughest test of self-esteem. But until we get out of our own way and start believing that *we are the beloved*, we'll continue to avoid suiting up and trusting our lives to the Lord. We will be driven and not called.

The minute you begin to think you can gain points with God by doing great things, you are straying off course. Humility brings you back.

Excellence

Most people think of excellence as being the best—better than anyone else. Unfortunately, there can only be one Number One. To think of excellence in this manner forces you to do those things that ultimately pull you away from God. It sets life up in a win-lose proposition where the only person that matters to you is good old Number One. But the kind of excellence that helps keep you on course is available to everyone. It's the process of rising up to the Lord's standard of excellence for you, which is nothing more and nothing less than you becoming the very best you that you can.

A number of years ago I spent a week with Rabbi Harold Kushner, the author of the best-selling book *When Bad Things Happen to Good People*. We were at a YPO University in Acapulco, and his presentation there was about a follow-up book, *When All You've Ever Wanted Is Not Enough*. From Rabbi Kushner I relearned that there are two acts in life: Achieve and Connect.

Act 1—achieve—is a natural act for human beings. After all, we are one of the only animals that can have goals outside of physical survival. Much of life for human beings today consists of, not just looking for and accumulating food or overcoming dangers to security, but also building and creating. Every freeway around a city on Monday morning is choked with thousands of people who are fulfilling their achieve act. The problem is that many people think that it's the only act in town. As a result, right up to their last breath these people are making life revolve around the next sale, the next triumph, the next victory. One of the hardest lessons for us to learn is that the person who dies with the most
50   toys does not win.

There is nothing wrong with achieving, for God put within us a desire to better ourselves and the world around us. The problems come when we put too much emphasis on achieving.

Richard N. Bolles, author of *What Color Is Your Parachute?* spoke to this in an interview entitled "Loving God and Loving Our Careers":

> If you show me someone who is enraptured by his or her work but has no religious convictions, I would be extremely pessimistic about trying to talk that individual out of basing his or her self-esteem too much on work performance. Unless a real crisis occurs in that person's life, and he or she becomes open, chances are there will be no change. That kind of absorption with one's career is almost like a drug. It's not just the job that strokes one's ego, it's the whole context of the work—fame, wealth, prestige, etc.—that reinforce overdependency on one's professional identity.

Rabbi Kushner says that in all his years as a rabbi he's never heard anyone say on their deathbed, "I wish I had gone to the office more." Instead, what do they wish? That they'd loved more, spent more time with family, friends, and loved ones. Most people never get beyond Act 1 in their lives.

Act 2—connect—is about relationships, the most important of which is your relationship to God. In Act 2, you realize it is important to connect with the Lord, with others, and with your own true self. Unfortunately, in our society few people think about Act 2 until they've had a mid-life crisis or a near-death experience. When tragedy strikes, they begin to raise questions about what life is really about, what it means. While it is never too late to open the curtain on Act 2, think of all you miss by waiting until something bad happens.

People who successfully move on to Act 2 are more likely to stay on course in their relationship to God. They also have a better chance of moving on to an integration of and a balance between achieving and connecting. Let's call that Act 3. When you define who you are by what it says on your business card, there isn't much, if any, room in your life for Act 2, and without Act 2, you can't go on to Act 3. An overemphasis on achievement makes it difficult to acknowledge grace because any thought about salvation or entry into heaven becomes another achievement. That leads to the "do" approach to religion, which leads to people dropping out because, in the end, you can never do enough.

Acknowledging grace requires that you accept that it is "done." You do not have to do anything more

because you cannot earn your way into acceptance. You

are already accepted. *You are already the beloved.* So now you can forget about trying to gain something for the sake of achievement and begin working at becoming the best person God intended you to be.

I love the story that Vernon Howard relates in his book, *The Mystic Path to Cosmic Power:*

> A prince was kidnapped at birth from his father's palace. Raised in poverty in a wretched village, he rebelled against the poverty of his life. He constructed careful plans for becoming king of the land. Through a series of schemes and battles, he won the throne. But he was anxious, hostile. Having taken the kingdom by force, he lived in dreaded fear of other ambitious men. It was day-to-day misery.
>
> Then he learned his true identity. He is a king by birthright. He sees the folly of trying to regain by force what is already his inheritance. Now, with his kingly consciousness, there is no fear, no threat, only quiet dominion.

Every one of us is a king or queen if we will only believe that *we are the beloved.* We don't need to be anything or anybody—we already are somebody. And no one can steal your throne from you with schemes or battles. It is yours as long as you want it.

In recent years I ask people in my management seminars, "How many of you have children?" Many hands go up. Then I ask, "How many of you love your children?" They laugh as the same hands go up. Then I raise the key question: "For how many of you is your love of your children dependent upon their achievements? If they are successful, you will love them. If they aren't, you won't." Not one hand ever goes up. "So love of your children does not depend on what they achieve or how much power or influence they gain," I continue. "And yet, why won't you and I accept that kind of unconditional love from our Father?"

Only when we do, according to Henri Nouwen, can we begin to hear our Father's comforting words:

> I hold you safe under My wings.
> You can come home always to Me
> whose name is Compassion!
> Whose name is Love!

> If you keep that image in mind—"that's where I belong"—you can live in the middle of this world and deal with enormous amounts of success as well as enormous amounts of failure without losing your identity. Because your identity is that *you are the beloved*.

I need a constant reminder that I am already loved or I can get caught in Act 1 like everyone else. After *The One Minute Manager* became successful, I then came out with *Putting the One Minute Manager to Work*, then *Leadership and the One Minute Manager*, then *The One Minute Manager Gets Fit*, and so on.

A friend of mine, Red Scott, brought me back down to earth when he said, "Blanchard, you caught lightning in the glass with *The One Minute Manager*. Enjoy it or you will spend the rest of your life trying to catch it again."

If we can begin to accept unconditional love from our Father, we set the stage for acknowledging grace. Your focus no longer has to be out there with results, accumulation, power, acceptance, control, or other earthly things. Now you can focus on your own sense of personal excellence and the journey—how to live your life. You can begin to live according to God's law.

"'Love the Lord your God with all your heart and with all your soul and with all your mind.' This is the first and greatest commandment, and the second is like it: 'Love your neighbor as yourself.' All the Law and the Prophets hang on these two commands" (Matthew 22:37–40).

Does this mean that achievement is bad? Absolutely not. Just don't focus on it as your reason for being. Amrit Desai says it well in John Scherer's wonderful little book *Work and the Human Spirit:* "The world is full of ego-giants who have found great success and great misery at the same time. There has never been a shortage of miserably rich, miserably successful people."

The emptiness and misery goes away when you have an inner peace that comes from accepting God's love and receiving His gift of grace. Your focus shifts from excelling in the eyes of others to excelling in the eyes of God. And the great irony is that when you acknowledge God's grace in your life, you get results— only now they come easier, and not by some sort of supernatural miracle in which God removes every barrier from your life. Think about it. Once you break out of the achievement game, you are free to do those things that you really like and to do them for the right reasons.

In recent years I have become friends with Larry Moody, director of Search Ministries. Besides helping business leaders with their walk with the Lord, Larry runs a Wednesday night Bible study on the PGA golf tour. Whenever I'm near a PGA event, I try to make it to Larry's Bible study. He's a marvelous preacher who has made a real difference in the lives of his golfing congregation, which includes, among others, Paul Azinger, Bernard Langer, Larry Mize, Larry Nelson, Corey Pavin, and Scott Simpson.

Larry teaches the meaning of grace to these players week after week. He emphasizes that whether they win or lose that week they are still loved. They can't win enough tournaments to get any more love or salvation. Given that, they might as well go out and play well since there is no "real pressure."

When "who you are" doesn't depend on your achievements and acceptance from others, does that make a difference? You bet! During the 1993 Masters, the last day of the tournament happened to fall on Easter Sunday. Beginning that day, Bernard Langer was leading the tournament. There's tremendous pressure on the leader of any tournament, much less the prestigious Masters.

Most golfers say it's much easier to be the challenger than the leader on the last day. When a leader loses, everyone talks about why that person choked. It took Nick Faldo years to overcome being called "Foldo" because he blew a number of tournaments. Lost tournaments have also haunted Greg Norman.

It was fun watching Langer on this special Sunday. He seemed to be what Chuck Hogan calls "mentally alert but physically relaxed." He seemed to be enjoying himself. When the "smart" decision would seem to be to play it safe (like his second shot on the famous par 5 thirteenth), he would go for it. He won the tournament by four strokes.

During the traditional interview of the winner by the president of Augusta National Golf Club, a comment was made about this being one of the greatest days of Bernard Langer's life. While Langer admitted winning the Masters was important, what was really special to him was "winning it on the anniversary of the resurrection of my Lord."

I'll never forget the comment Tom Landry, the legendary Dallas Cowboys coach, made when he was asked how he was able to remain so calm on the field no matter what happened: "It's easy because I have my priorities in order. First comes my Lord, second comes my wife, then comes my kids, and finally my job. If I lose on Sunday I have a lot left over."

That hit me like a thunderbolt; I knew it was not true with most people, including myself at times. So many of us think life is all about winning. But I like the words of the late tennis star Arthur Ashe: "True heroism is remarkably sober, very undramatic. It's not the urge to surpass all others at whatever cost, but the urge to serve others at whatever cost."

Am I suggesting that if you acknowledge God's grace in your life that you'll be a star athlete or winning football coach? Not at all. But as these men each shared in their own way, putting God first takes the pressure to perform off your shoulders, and most of the time, that allows us to be the best person God intended us to be. That's the kind of excellence that keeps us on course.

I'm writing a book on winning values and coaching with Don Shula, legendary coach of the Miami Dolphins and the winningest coach in NFL history. Don's favorite saying is "success is not forever and failure isn't fatal." He feels strongly that you can't afford to be overconfident in victory or be consumed by failure. Don goes to mass every morning he possibly can to give thanks and ask for help. While he wants to win—and there's nobody more competitive than he is—his faith keeps winning and losing in perspective. For over thirty years Don has not only won a minimum of ten games a season, but he has kept the Lord and his family at the top of his priorities.

Whenever you're tempted to veer off course and try to make a name for yourself, remember that if you go it alone you're bound to get caught in the achievement game—a game you can never win. Focus instead on becoming excellent in God's eyes and enjoy the blessings that follow.

Listening

One of my teachers used to say: "If God had wanted us to talk more than listen, He would have given us two mouths." One reason we have trouble staying on course and trusting God's grace is that we don't take time to quiet ourselves and listen to the Lord. We are undisciplined in "inner listening." Henri Nouwen suggests that in spiritual terms, discipline is creating some space for God—space where God can act, speak, and let something happen that surprises us and lets us know He is there. This means that we have to stop filling up all our time or being preoccupied in the time we have alone.

Why is solitude so hard for us? In our collaboration, Norman Vincent Peale and I realized that we all have two selves: an inner self that is thoughtful, reflective, and a good listener; and an outer, task-oriented self that is focused on achieving and often too busy to learn. The latter self is what drives us in Act 1, the act of achieving. The attention of the inner self is on Act 2 and Act 3—connecting with people and finding significance in life. It is the vehicle we have that helps us listen to the Lord—the caller—and makes sure we are living according to God's purpose for us.

The problem is that it takes longer to awaken our inner self in the morning. When the alarm goes off, most of us leap out of bed into our task-oriented selves without giving our inner selves a thought. We eat while we wash and then we're off to our first meeting or activity of the day. We race around from one thing to another, with lunch and dinner squeezed in somewhere. At the end of the day, we fall exhausted into bed with hardly enough energy to say goodnight to the loved one lying next to us. The next day is more of the same. Pretty soon, one day leads into another, and life becomes little more than a blur. As Lily Tomlin used to say, "The trouble with being in a rat race is that even if you win the race, you're still a rat."

The way to avoid the rat race and stay on course is to honor the inner self by seeking solitude—times when we can be "alone with God, and God alone."

Why is solitude so important in keeping you on your journey? Henri Nouwen says it well:

> Because it's the place where you can listen to the voice of the One who calls you *the beloved*. That's what prayer is all about. To pray is to listen to the voice of the One who calls you *my beloved daughter, my beloved son, my beloved child*. To pray is to let that voice speak to the center of your being— to your guts. And let that voice resonate in your whole being. Who am I? *I am the beloved.*

How can you find time for solitude? I recommend you enter your day more slowly. People have talked about quiet time with the Lord in the morning for years, whether it be called "the morning watch" or special time for "personal devotions." Let me share what has worked for me, but also confess that it takes discipline. I must admit I don't do what I describe every day. It's stupid but true. It's good old free will in action again. My hunch is that all of us have the same problem—we know we need to spend more time in quiet reflection, but we let other things crowd that time. Maybe that's why mornings work best for me. When I am being really good to myself, I try to make quiet time the first priority of the day before anything else, like a phone call, has a chance to interfere.

When my day starts off well, one of the first things I do is sit quietly and relax. After some deep breathing, I begin doing some stretching to help rehabilitate a couple of nagging injuries to my left hip and knee. I mention stretching because, while I'm on my back working on my flexibility, it's a perfect time to pray and listen.

I start my prayers with a Psalm: "This is the day the Lord hath made. Let us rejoice and be glad in it."

From Bob Buford, I learned to pray in four areas depicted by the acronym ACTS:

Adoration. This is where all prayers should begin—telling the Lord that you love Him and appreciate all He has done and created.

> Yours, Oh LORD,
> is the greatness and power
> and the glory and the majesty
> and the splendor,
> for everything in heaven and earth is yours.
> Yours, Oh LORD, is the kingdom;
> you are exalted as head over all.
> —(1 Chronicles 29:11)

Confession. Since we still fall short of God's perfection, we need to make sure we are cleansed of every sin we have committed.

> If we confess our sins,
> he is faithful and just
> and will forgive us our sins,
> and purify us from all unrighteousness.
> —(1 John 1:9)

Thanksgiving. I think one of the reasons why Thanksgiving Day is such a treasured holiday is that we truly enjoy being thankful. So why not do it every day?

During this part of my prayer I thank God specifically for all that he did for me since the last time we talked.

> Sing and make music in your heart to the Lord,
> always giving thanks to God the Father
> for everything, in the name
> of our Lord Jesus Christ.
> —(Ephesians 5:19–20)

Supplication. This is just another word for asking for what you need. I like to start with prayers for others and then ask for my own needs to be met. I have a big "wish list." My biggest wish is to give myself and the people I love the strength to proclaim, "Not what *I* want but *Thy* will be done on earth as it is in heaven." According to God's Word, we can ask with confidence:

> Ask and it will be given to you;
> seek and you will find;
> knock and the door will be
> opened to you.
> —(Matthew 7:7)

Bill Hybels suggested I write my prayers down because I would be amazed at how many come true. When I do that in a journal it helps me to remember my blessings and how much the Lord listens.

During my prayer time, I always spend a few moments in silence, listening. Now, you may have heard a preacher say, "God told me . . ." and wondered what he was talking about. He gives the impression that God speaks to him directly in a clear, loud voice. I admit that I have not been on this journey long enough to know all the answers, but I have to confess I have never heard God speak in an audible voice. Yet I'd also have to say I am convinced I have heard from God. Usually, when I am quiet before Him, my thoughts are directed to those things He wants me to think about or do. That's when it is particularly important to listen.

God also speaks through His Word, the Bible. Keith Jackson, the Miami Dolphins' All-Pro tight end, who sometimes leads a Bible study for his teammates calls the Bible, "**B**asic **I**nstruction **B**efore **L**eaving **E**arth." That's a humorous way to remember that God inspired writers to preserve His teachings so that we would know how to live. Spending time each day reading the Bible gives you direct access to God. It is more than a reading assignment; it is a way to understand how God wants you to live. I seldom come away from reading the Bible without learning some important nugget of truth about my journey.

Listening, for me, also includes reading other helpful devotional books. In addition to reading the Bible each morning, I usually read a selection from a daily devotional—a collection of inspirational readings designed to be read through in a year. My current favorites are *Time With God* and *The Daily Word* (a monthly publication my mother has given me since I was a child), but there are many wonderful ones on the market.

On an ideal day, when I am finished praying and reading, I end my time of solitude before God by doing some exercise. A lot of people exercise for their physical health, not realizing that it's also good for their spiritual health as well. As one who believes God made me, I think it is important to take care of my body even though I often don't act that way. The Bible calls the body the "temple of the Lord," and I need to be good to this old temple. But I also know that during my daily walk I can continue listening to God.

Here again, we need to be careful about treating exercise as another achievement. Some people turn running or biking or some other good form of activity into a religion. They measure their performances and get down on themselves when they don't measure up. A dear friend of mine, Jim Ballad, has been a morning jogger for over twenty years. I love to be around Jim when people ask him how far he runs every day. His reply is "I don't know."

They usually counter with, "Well, how long do you jog each day?"

Again, Jim will say, "I don't know. My jogging is not about getting anywhere. It's just the way I choose to enter my day."

What a great approach to exercise. And what a great way to listen. A morning walk helps keep me on course on my journey.

Any effort to quiet yourself through prayer, reading, or any other solitary activity is part of what Rick Warren, pastor of Saddleback Community Church in Orange County, California calls going from first base to second. Rick depicts the spiritual journey of a Christian like the four bases on a baseball field. Rick says that acknowledging God's grace by confessing our sins puts us on first base. The trip to second and third base involves growing in our knowledge of Christ and serving Him. We round third and head for home when we are able to share our faith comfortably with others on a consistent basis.

Last year Margie made it to first base after reading Robert Laidlow's *The Reason Why* during a ski trip to Aspen with a group of old Cornell friends. The year before, she had hurt her leg skiing, so she decided to take it easy on this trip. Phil Hodges gave Laidlow's little booklet to Margie to read when we all headed off to the slopes.

When I got back to the room at the end of our ski day, Margie said, "Well, I did it!"

I said, "Did what?"

"I suited up," she smiled. "They ask for a decision at the end of the booklet Hodge gave me, so I bowed my head and did it."

What a great day that was for me! You suit up one at a time. Margie is not an emotional decision maker like I am. She is much more thoughtful. She had to suit up on her own timetable. But now we are really on the same team—forever!

The following Saturday we had dinner with Bob Buford. When Margie told Bob what she had done, he began to cry and ran over to give her a big hug.

Margie said to him, "But I still have a lot of questions."

Bob said, "That's great! Now that you are on first base you should ask plenty of questions. You are ready to head to second base."

According to Warren, once you have committed to membership in God's family, you are ready to head to second base and develop your spiritual maturity by becoming a hearer of the Word—a student of the Bible.

This journey we are on is about growing in Christ. This is why solitude is so important.

When fog settles in over a seaport, ships listen for the foghorn to know where the dangers are. The sound of the horn helps them stay on course. We too need to listen so that we don't stray off course. The old habit of charging hard through life leaves little time for listening to the voice that calls us to a more excellent way. I am at my best when I start each day quietly before the Lord, talking to Him and listening for His reply.

Praising

Of all the concepts I have taught managers over the years, the most important has been the power of praising. Spencer Johnson and I emphasized in *The One Minute Manager* that the key to developing people is to catch them doing something right so you can pat them on the back and recognize their performance. Nothing motivates people more than being caught in the act of doing something right. If you are to stay on course in your walk with God, you need to begin to do the same thing with yourself.

When was the last time you caught yourself doing something right? Unless you're unusual, you find it hard to praise yourself. Most of the time, you catch yourself doing things wrong, and then feel badly about it. No wonder we have a hard time feeling as if *we are the beloved*.

Recognizing the difficulty of receiving praise, Margie and I went out of our way to teach our kids, Scott and Debbie, to become comfortable with receiving compliments. In fact, we taught them to follow a word of praise with the affirmation, "Thanks for noticing." I'll never forget the time friends arrived for a visit one day before Margie and I had gotten home from work. Scott, who was a teenager at the time, was there to greet them. He showed them to their room, got them something to drink, and generally entertained them. When we got home they praised Scott for his hospitality in front of us. He said, "Thanks for noticing. It's important to me that Mom and Dad's friends and my friends feel at home here." Is it any wonder that Scott ended up going to the Hotel School at Cornell and studying the hospitality business?

When it comes to catching yourself doing things right, praising is all about self-talk. A number of years ago I cofounded the Golf University in San Diego with a top teaching professional. The reason I got involved in such a venture is that not only am I a golf fanatic, but I think golf is the closest to life of any sport. In fact, I say golf stands for **Game Of Life First**.

In most sports, you are reacting to someone else. If that person is bigger, faster, stronger, or better than you are, it's hard for you to compete. In golf, you don't react to anyone else. That little white ball sits there and waits for you to hit it. And sometimes in golf you are hitting it better than you should and you have to deal with success. At other times, you hit it worse than you should and must deal with failure. In golf, like life, you get good breaks and bad ones you don't deserve as well as ones you do deserve, and you must deal with all of this in four and a half hours. I can learn more about someone in one round of golf than working with them for a long period of time. Golf brings out the best and worst in people.

At our Golf University we not only teach people the mechanical side of the game—how to hit the golf ball in different situations—but the mental side as well. On that side of things we focus on self-talk because that part of the game is usually negative with most players. Most golfers beat themselves up on the golf course. I played with a fellow once who yelled at himself, "You idiot! How can you be so stupid?" almost before he hit the ball. No matter how he shot, it wasn't good enough. I suggested he quit the game since it seemed to cause him such grief. My fear is that he lives his life the same way—always finding fault with himself.

If you're going to stay on course in your journey, you need to focus on catching yourself doing something right. How do you get started? Bill Hybels gave me a marvelous suggestion in his book *Honest to God*. For a long time people had told him he should keep a journal. But being competitive, he was always sidetracked by trying to think how he could write a better journal than anyone else. And yet he knew people who wrote in their journals in four colors. Others wrote poems in their journals and the like. So he never got around to keeping a journal because he knew it would never be the best. Then he became the chaplain for the Chicago Bears.

Every Monday morning he would conduct a Bible study for some of the players and staff. After the Bible study the team always watched the game films from the weekend game. They would watch for things they did well and could feel good about as well as the things they did poorly and needed to improve upon. One day when Bill was heading back to his church, it hit him like a thunderbolt. "That's it!" he thought. "That's how to write a journal."

His thought was to write the word *Yesterday* at the top of the page and then relive the day before in terms of things he did or thought that he felt good about and the things he would like to live over. Now his journal was unique to him, and he would be able to keep his ego from letting his journal be a competitive game.

Keeping a journal that monitors yesterday's triumphs sets you up for self-praise. When I do my "yesterday" journal, I start by catching myself doing things right. What did I do yesterday that makes me proud? What did I do that glorifies the Lord's name and shows that I found His love? For example, I am working on my language during my speeches and seminars. When I get excited about something, my language can get colorful. Over the years I have gotten some negative feedback about it but had never really committed to improving this behavior until I suited up. It suddenly became apparent that my use of four-letter words didn't add a thing to my sessions, and it certainly didn't glorify the Lord's name. Besides, it set up an incongruity if I hoped to witness about the power of the Lord in my life.

Once I committed to improving my language, do you think the change happened overnight? Absolutely not! Changing past behavior is not easy because you develop habit patterns that encourage you to do certain things without even thinking. Keeping a journal has been helpful in tracking my progress. It helps me catch myself doing something right, allowing myself to pat myself on the back with a word of praise.

When you are learning to do something new—or in my case, unlearning a past behavior—you can't wait until you do it exactly right before you praise yourself. You have to praise progress because it is a moving target. Exactly right behavior is made up of a series of approximately right behaviors. So be kind to yourself. If you're not your own best friend, who will be?

What if I didn't make any progress? How would I record that in my journal? I would redirect myself. That means I would go back to goal-setting and check my commitment. Self-praise should never prevent you from honestly evaluating your commitment to changing a negative behavior. Sometimes I need to reprimand myself in my journal, but I do it and I don't dwell on it. That helps keep my mistakes in perspective: "I'm okay, it's just my behavior that's a problem sometimes. God didn't make junk. He just made real people who have behavior problems from time to time."

While keeping a journal is an excellent way to keep track of the things you do that are praiseworthy, there are other ways to praise yourself. Mostly it's a mindset—thinking more about the good that you do than the bad. It means recognizing that for the most part, we really do try to spend more time lighting candles than cursing the darkness. It's just that it's so easy

to get into the habit of focusing on your mistakes. The

more you do that, the easier it is to stray off course and begin thinking you're all alone. That you need to do something great to earn your way into acceptance.

Remember, *you are already loved.*

DESTINATIONS

I pray that you,
being rooted and established in love,
may have power, together
with all the saints, to grasp
how wide and long and high and
deep is the love of Christ.

EPHESIANS 3:17–18

have been traveling on this wonderful spiritual journey now for almost ten years. You would think that by now I would have arrived, or at least be very close to arriving. But arriving implies a specific destination, and to most people the final destination is where we spend eternity. One of the paradoxes of faith is that the closer you get to understanding issues of life after death, the less it matters. In other words, because I believe that God has prepared a place for me after I leave this world, I worry less about it than ever before. Some theologians and scholars have tried to describe heaven. Frankly, I don't think about it much. All I know is that it will be perfect because I will be in God's presence forever.

So where am I going? What is the destination of my journey with God? Why try to stay on course?

I believe the only destination that matters for now is the life God has given us to live—here and now. You've probably heard the saying, "He was so heavenly minded that he was no earthly good." It refers to people

79

that focus so much on heaven that they forget about their earthly destinations. What a shame to acknowledge the gift of grace and go on living as if nothing were different.

When God gets our attention and we accept His grace and forgiveness, our feet are set on a new path. My brief prayer inviting God to enter my life was really only the beginning of my journey. It gave me new priorities and a new way of looking at myself. Although I'm still the same person with the same talents He gave me, I now see that I can use those talents to bring glory to His name. And in the process, I am able to become the best person I can be.

Your new destination, then, is really a new purpose in life. By purpose, I mean your reason for being—something toward which you are always striving. A purpose is different than a goal in that it does not have a beginning or an end—it is ongoing. It gives meaning and definition to our lives.

In *The Power of Ethical Management,* Norman Vincent Peale and I talked about purpose as a particular road you choose to travel. A goal is one of the places you intend to visit on that road. So while making money is a goal we can strive for, it is not our purpose in life, although some people act like it is and put all their energy into accumulating cash and assets.

Purpose is not about any achievement, it is bigger. It's your calling—deciding what kind of business you are in as a person.

Having a clear purpose makes it easier to accept God's gift of grace and continue to trust it. After all, if we talk about your "calling," we must also talk about the "caller." It does not seem reasonable to work on a personal mission statement without dealing with your relationship to the Lord, because they are so interrelated. Acknowledging God's grace sends you off on a journey to wholeness. God already made up the difference between you and 100 and now wants you to live as close to an integrated life (Act 3) as possible—a balance between achieving and connecting.

So while we still have the gift of life, our destination as followers of God is to have a clear sense of purpose in serving Him. One of the best ways to do this is to borrow the concept of a mission statement from the business world and develop your own. Have you ever done that?

Richard Bolles, in his essay entitled *How to Find Your Mission in Life*, helped me a great deal in writing a personal mission statement. He says that part of everyone's mission statement ought to include "making the world a better place to live." Sounds simple, doesn't it? I ask folks at my seminars, "How many of you would like to make the world a better place?" All hands go up. Then I ask, "How are you accomplishing that?" The room usually goes silent. While everyone would like to make the world better, they usually don't know how to get started.

Bolles has a wonderful strategy. He says you can make the world a better place by the moment-by-moment decisions you make in your interactions with the people with whom you come in contact. He suggests that every time you interact with someone, whether a loved one, a friend, or a person you meet in the street, you have a choice—to add more love to the world or less, more honesty or less, more forgiveness or less, or more gratitude or less, or more justice or less.

Suppose you're driving down the highway. Someone on your right is in the wrong lane and obviously needs to get back into your lane. *Choice point:* do you add more forgiveness to the world or less? Do you smile and slow down to let that person into your lane, or do you give that person a dirty look (or worse) and step on the gas?

Suppose your spouse yells at you as you're leaving the house. *Choice point:* do you add more love to the world or less? Do you go back into the house and give your spouse a hug and say, "I hope your day goes better," or do you yell back and pour fuel on the fire?

I think you get the point. Once you suit up on God's team, your purpose changes from serving yourself to serving others, and your personal mission statement ought to reflect that.

Another aspect of your mission statement has to do with your *calling*. I've heard of people who suited up and then left successful careers to become ministers or missionaries. I have nothing against that kind of work, but the Bible tells us that everyone in the family of God is a minister—we just do not necessarily have to run a church or move to another country.

God has given you a unique set of gifts. He wired you a certain way. He didn't put you here to keep fighting your weaknesses. What you love to do is probably what you ought to be doing. So as you think about your mission statement, ask yourself this question: "What do I love to do?"

Every once in a while I put my arm around a manager and tell that person, "You're going to be all right. In fact, you're a beautiful person, but the Lord didn't put you on earth to manage others." Some people often make excellent individual contributors, but they don't have the listening, supporting, or facilitating characteristics to help someone else.

I recognized early on in my career that the Lord didn't put me on earth to manage others. Harry Evarts, who retired a few years ago from a top management position with the American Management Association (AMA), laughs whenever he sees me. My first job out of graduate school was working for him as his administrative assistant when he was dean of the College of Business Administration at Ohio University. We can't decide whether he fired me before I quit, or I quit before he fired me. It probably was a photo finish.

At any rate, I was a terrible administrator. With the exception of my secretary, Eleanor Terndrup, no one in our company (BTD) reports to me. And since I travel so much, Eleanor is not quite sure who she reports to either. But we've been together for over fifteen years, so it all works out.

I got some additional help in writing my mission statement from Tony Robbins, the personal growth guru and best-selling author of *Unlimited Power* and *Awake the Giant Within*. Now, I realize some of my Christian friends worry about my relationship with Tony because they do not think he is a believer. But I believe God loves Tony Robbins, and I am delighted with the increased spiritual emphasis in his teaching. He has been receptive to listening to my journey of faith, and I continue to support his search for Truth.

During "A Date with Destiny," Tony told us to write and rewrite our personal mission statements until we could tell others our mission with real passion and commitment. I wrote: "I am a loving teacher of simple truths who helps myself and others to awaken the presence of God in our lives."

When I began to share this with others, I made one change. I added "and example," so that it now reads: "I am a loving teacher *and example* of simple truths who helps myself and others awaken the presence of God in our lives." Spencer Johnson gave me the new suggested words because he said he knows a lot of people who don't practice what they preach. That certainly includes me from time to time. That's why the pressure to set an example is important.

The reason I made "awaken the presence of God in our lives" part of my mission statement is that I feel the biggest addiction we have in the world today is the human ego. If I can help myself and others to awaken the presence of God in our lives, we have a better chance to get out of our own way, get to know God better, receive grace, and make the world a better place. I say "we" because I am on the same journey.

What is your mission statement—your reason for being? If you're having trouble with that question, you might try an interesting activity that may help you develop a clear sense of purpose: write your own obituary. This gives you a chance—ahead of time—to describe the ideal you. What would you look like? How would you behave? What would you be remembered for?

I first got interested in writing my own obituary when I heard a story about Alfred Nobel, the originator of the Nobel Peace Prize. His brother died at the turn of the century, and when Alfred got a copy of the newspaper to see what was said about his brother, he was shocked to discover the paper had mixed him up with his brother. So he got to read his own obituary.

When he was younger, Alfred had been involved in the invention of dynamite. What do you think his obituary was all about? Dynamite and destruction.

Nobel was devastated. When he talked with his friends and loved ones about what had happened, they asked, "What is the opposite of destruction? Peace!" So Nobel redesigned his life so he would be remembered for peace.

What would you like to be remembered for? How do you picture your life?

Here's what I would like my obituary to read:

Ken Blanchard was a loving teacher and example of simple truths whose books and lectures on leadership and management helped himself and others awaken the presence of God in their lives. He was a caring spouse, father, friend, and colleague who strove to find a balance between achievement and relationships. He had a spiritual peace about him that permitted him to say no in a loving manner to people and projects that got him off purpose. He was a person of high energy who was able to see the positive in any event. No matter what happened he could find a lesson or message in it. Ken Blanchard was someone who trusted God's unconditional love and believed he was *the beloved*. He valued integrity and walked his talk. He was a mean and lean 185-pound flexible machine who won the Seniors Golf Championship at his club when he was well into his seventies with his wife Margie walking the whole way at his side. He will be missed because wherever he went he made the world a better place for his having been there.

Okay, maybe I got a little carried away with the weight and golfing, but why not? Margie says, "A goal is a dream with a deadline." When you write your obituary before you die, it is a dream—a big picture goal of what you want your life to be and mean. Don't hold back. Don't think of your lesser self but your best self, for that is what God intended you to be all along. And don't do it alone. Quiet yourself, pray, and listen to the voice that says, "You are loved." Once you know what your purpose is in life, is there any way to monitor your behavior to make sure you live "on purpose"? The "yesterday" journal I referred to earlier is a very powerful way to keep yourself on track. When I have written in my journal it forces me to take a good hard look at my behavior.

Keeping a journal that monitors your yesterdays also sets up your prayers. It highlights what you are thankful for and pinpoints areas for which you might need to ask forgiveness. For years my mother has said, "There are two phrases we don't use enough in life: 'Thank you' and 'I'm sorry.'"

Giving thanks is tough enough, but saying "I'm sorry" is extremely difficult for the human ego. We're reluctant to admit we're wrong and ask forgiveness.

I'll never forget a letter I got a number of years ago from a top manager at Honeywell. He had just read *The One Minute Manager*. He said he liked the three secrets—*One Minute Goal Setting*, *One Minute Praisings*, and *One Minute Reprimands*—but they all assumed that managers are always right. And yet, managers are often wrong. He suggested the fourth secret of *The One Minute Manager* should be the *One Minute Apology*.

That really made sense to me and I have shared the *One Minute Apology* with people everywhere I go. Still, it is hard for all of us. Even if you didn't read the book *Love Story* or see the movie, I'll bet you can recall the saying that became famous from Eric Segal's story: "Love is never having to say you're sorry." People thought that was a wonderful saying. When you think about it, that is an awful saying. I think we should rewrite it to say: "Love is being able to say you're sorry!" That's more like it. So keeping a "yesterday" journal can help keep you on track and re-route you if you get off purpose.

Some final thoughts

Well, that's all the advice I have to help you accept, receive, and trust God's unconditional love. This little book has been my attempt to share Christ—what Rick Warren describes as the journey from third base to home. This is my mission in the world: being a doer and not just a hearer of God's Word.

I admit I may be getting a little ahead of myself. Bill Hybels told me he prays for me all the time because, "Blanchard, with a little knowledge, you could be dangerous." If I hear something new, I'm likely to lecture about it the next day. I may be new in the faith, but I really want to tell you about it.

I hope you have enjoyed this book and found something of value in it. I have! I needed this message and the reminder to rely on H.E.L.P. as much as anyone. While I've accepted grace, I still have to awaken constantly to the presence of God in my life so I will trust His unconditional love.

But I don't want to let you off the hook. Are *you* ready to suit up? Are *you* ready to receive God's unconditional love and accept His Son as your Savior? If you are, all you have to do is say and believe these words:

> Lord, I come to You as a sinner—I fall short of Your perfection. I realize I cannot save myself. I need Your help. I *accept Jesus Christ into my life as my Savior and Lord.* I humbly accept Your gift of grace, Your gift of salvation.

If you just suited up or were already on the team, great! If you didn't, you may be asking, "Is Jesus the only way to salvation and a better life on earth?"

I raised that very question one time with Norman Vincent Peale. I asked him, "Do you believe Jesus is *the* Truth and *the* Way?"

He said "Absolutely!"

"But what about the millions of people who never heard about Jesus?" I wondered. "Or the millions of good people who heard about Him but decided not to follow Him?"

Norman smiled and said, "I believe in a loving God. I'll bet He handles that in a loving way. I'm in sales, not management."

While I like Norman's answer, I hope this question will never be a big issue for you, because you realize there is no better deal than Christianity.

As you move from accepting to trusting, don't be too hard on yourself. It's not always easy to walk with Jesus. Those earthly voices you've listened to all your life can still get you off course. Keep seeking the H.E.L.P. you need—strive for *humility*, focus on your own *excellence*, not just achievement, keep *listening* to the voice that says, "You are the beloved," and *praise* your progress.

Every journey begins with a single step, and moves along one step at a time.

Enjoy the trip!

Acknowledgments

First of all, I want to thank my partner Margie, son Scott, and daughter Debbie for putting up with all my verbal and written spiritual ramblings and encouraging me to share them more widely. Their journey with the Lord is moving forward at different speeds but based on the belief that they are *beloved*.

I am also indebted to many friends and colleagues who gave me feedback on this little book. In particular, I want to thank Jim Ballard and Sheldon Bowles for their very thoughtful and thorough feedback. It added a great deal to this final version.

A special thanks to my longtime secretary and friend Eleanor Terndrup and recent colleague David Wilt for preparing and typing the various versions of this manuscript with love, patience, and skill.

Margaret McBride, my literary agent and friend, was there once again to give me love, encouragement, and an "all-win" contract.

Lyn Cryderman, senior acquisitions editor at Zondervan Publishing House, was marvelous. He came to our cottage in upstate New York, plugged in his Macintosh, rolled up his sleeves, and spent two days with me finalizing the manuscript. I feel like I've known him forever.

And finally, I want to acknowledge my three-member consulting team—the Father, the Son, and the Holy Ghost—for the new energy and purpose they have given my life. I only hope I have represented them well.

Bibliography

Blanchard, Kenneth and Norman Vincent Peale. *The Power of Ethical Management*. New York: William Morrow & Co., 1988.

___, and Spencer Johnson. *The One-Minute Manager*. New York: William Morrow & Co., 1982.

Bolles, Richard N. *What Color Is Your Parachute?* Berkeley, CA: Ten Speed Press, 1991.

___. *How to Find Your Mission in Life*. Berkeley, CA: Ten Speed Press, 1991.

___. "Loving God and Loving Our Careers" was an interview of Richard Bolles that appeared in "Crossings," a newsletter published by the Church of Divinity School of the Pacific, 1989.

Bright, Bill. *Four Spiritual Laws*. Arrowhead Springs, San Bernadino, CA: Campus Crusade for Christ International, 1965.

Canfield, Jack, and Mark Victor Hansen. *Chicken Soup for the Soul*. Deerfield Beach, FL: Health Communications, Inc., 1993. I first read the "Sachi story" in this book. It originally came from page 48 of Dan Millman's book *Sacred Journey of the Peaceful Warrior*. Tiburon, CA: H. J. Kramer, Inc., 1983.

Crum, Thomas F. *The Magic of Conflict*. New York: Simon & Schuster, 1988.

Hogan, Chuck. *Five Days to Golfing Excellence*. Sedona, AZ: T & C Publishing, 1986.

Howard, Vernon. *The Mystic Path of Cosmic Power*. Ojai, CA: New Life Foundation, 1988.

Hybels, Bill. *Honest to God?* Grand Rapids: Zondervan, 1992.

___. *Seven Wonders of the Spiritual World*. Irving, TX: Word, 1988.

Krushner, Harold S. *When Bad Things Happen to Good People*. Boston: G. K. Hall, 1982.

___. *When All You've Ever Wanted Isn't Enough*. Boston: G. K. Hall, 1987.

Laidlaw, Robert A. *The Reason Why*. Chattanooga, TN: CBMC Publications.

MacDonald, Byron is the pastor at Rolling Hills Covenant Church in North Rolling Hills Estates, California. Phil Hodges sends me a tape of MacDonald's sermon each week—he is a marvelous preacher. On one of these tapes, I heard the story about the rabbi who wanted to change the city.

MacDonald, Gordon. *Ordering Your Private World*. Nashville: Oliver-Nelson, 1985.

Nouwen, Henri J. M. and his thinking were introduced to me by Bob Buford. He sent me a tape of Nouwen's talk entitled "Solitude, Community, and Ministry" at the 1993 Foundation Conference for Christian Business Leaders in Toronto. After I finished the first draft of *We Are the Beloved*, a colleague found Nouwen's latest book, *Life of the Beloved* (New York: Crossroad, 1992). Nouwen's work inspired the title for this book.

Robbins, Anthony. *Unlimited Power*. New York: Fawcett Books, 1987.

___. *Awaken the Giant Within*. New York: Summit, 1991.

Scherer, John, with Larry Shook. *Work and the Human Spirit*. Spokane, WA: John Scherer & Associates, 1993.

Warren, Rick. Rick is the dynamic minister at Saddleback Valley Community Church in Southern California. Bob Buford shared with me Rick's approach to the spiritual journey of a Christian.

Zuck, Colleen (ed.). *The Daily Word*. Unity Village, MO: School of Christianity.